T0407078

Showdown

The Fight for Space

Dona Herweck Rice

Consultant

William B. Rice
Engineering Geologist

Publishing Credits

Rachelle Cracchiolo, *M.S.Ed., Publisher*
Conni Medina, M.A.Ed., *Managing Editor*
Nika Fabienke, Ed.D., *Series Developer*
June Kikuchi, *Content Director*
Seth Rogers, *Editor*
Michelle Jovin, M.A., *Assistant Editor*
Kevin Pham, *Graphic Designer*

TIME For Kids and the TIME For Kids logo are registered trademarks of TIME Inc. Used under license.

Image Credits: p.11 (inset) Andrey Nekrasov/Alamy Stock Photo; p.12 (inset) age fotostock/Alamy Stock Photo; pp.16-17 Nature Picture Library/Alamy Stock Photo; pp.22-23 Illustrations by Timothy J. Bradley; p.30 (inset) Rosanne Tackaberry/Alamy Stock Photo; pp.36-37 Jeffrey L. Rotman/Getty Images; all other images from iStock and/or Shutterstock.

All companies and products mentioned in this book are registered trademarks of their respective owners or developers and are used in this book strictly for editorial purposes; no commercial claim to their use is made by the author or the publisher.

Library of Congress Cataloging-in-Publication Data

Names: Rice, Dona, author.
Title: Showdown : the fight for space / Dona Herweck Rice.
Description: Huntington Beach, CA : Teacher Created Materials, [2018] | Audience: Grade 4 to 6. | Includes index.
Identifiers: LCCN 2017023528 (print) | LCCN 2017030010 (ebook) | ISBN 9781425854676 (eBook) | ISBN 9781425849917 (pbk.)
Subjects: LCSH: Animal behavior--Juvenile literature. | Animals--Habitations--Juvenile literature.
Classification: LCC QL751.5 (ebook) | LCC QL751.5 .R55 2018 (print) | DDC 591.5--dc23
LC record available at https://lccn.loc.gov/2017023528

Teacher Created Materials

5301 Oceanus Drive
Huntington Beach, CA 92649-1030
http://www.tcmpub.com
ISBN 978-1-4258-4991-7
© 2018 Teacher Created Materials, Inc.
Made in China
Nordica.092017.CA21701119

Table of Contents

There Once Was a Town

There once was a young town in the low, green hills of the West. People moved there from the big cities and areas already heavy with population. They wanted to live among the open hillsides and old farmlands. They liked the wild, natural spaces that still existed amid the new homes and businesses. The people who were not used to the natural world at their doorsteps thought they had found a paradise. In many ways, they had.

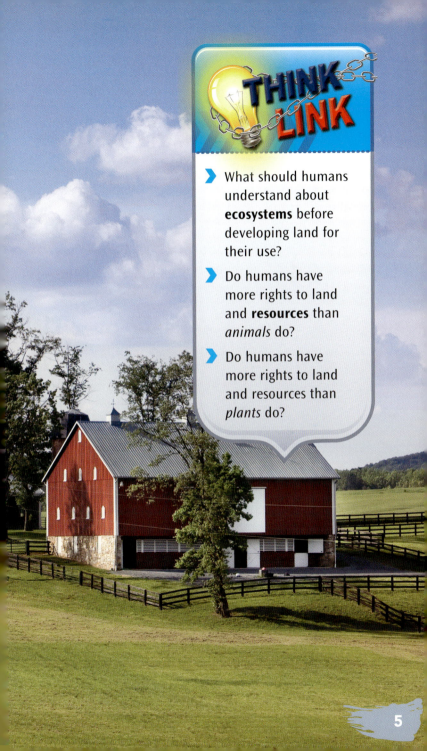

- What should humans understand about **ecosystems** before developing land for their use?

- Do humans have more rights to land and **resources** than *animals* do?

- Do humans have more rights to land and resources than *plants* do?

Life seemed perfect for the people in the town. There was just one problem. Others already lived on the land. Animals large and small had made this place their home for many years, and they had nowhere else to go. Looking for open land and resources, the animals shared the humans' new space.

Coyotes hunted as they always did, but their **prey** now included the small pets of the families living there. Snakes sometimes coiled in backyards under hoses and barbecue grills, looking for shelter and warmth. And in the dark of night, mice, possums, and skunks wandered free and enjoyed the fruits of family gardens.

Pet Protection

In areas where people live close to nature, they must protect their pets. Foxes and other animals that hunt find their next meals wherever they can. Small dogs and cats left unattended can become prey.

Spiders: Friends or Foes?

Living closely with nature means living with spiders—and that's a good thing! Spiders help maintain the population of insects. But some spiders are dangerous to humans. A harmful black widow might be found in a backyard wood stack as easily as a harmless jumping spider hiding behind curtains.

Relationships Among Species

It is important to understand what happens when different species **vie** for the same resources. To do this, you must first understand the ways species interact. Every species is, at any given time, doing its best to survive. Each species lives by **instinct** and nature. These things work together to keep the species alive and healthy. The instinct to survive is strong.

Most species do not make a plan for living side by side with other species. Only humans can do that. Whether humans actually make a plan is another story.

Growth and Changes

Growth and changes in a species is impacted most by changes in their environment. Changes in **habitat** and climate play a role, too. So do the ways in which species interact with each other. These changes can affect entire ecosystems.

Community

When two or more species interact in a given place, it is known as an *ecological community*. What one species does affects the other. Species in the same place do not exist apart from one another. Instead, they depend on each other to survive.

There are four basic relationships that species can have. Each type has to do with the way in which species interact. The relationships are mutualism, commensalism, predation, and competition.

Mutualism

Mutualism is when both sides benefit. Each side gives, and each side receives. Neither is harmed; both are helped.

Bees and flowers practice mutualism. Bees gather nectar from flowers. The nectar becomes their food. Bees also carry pollen from flower to flower. In this way, they assist the flowers' **reproduction**. The existence of each depends on the other.

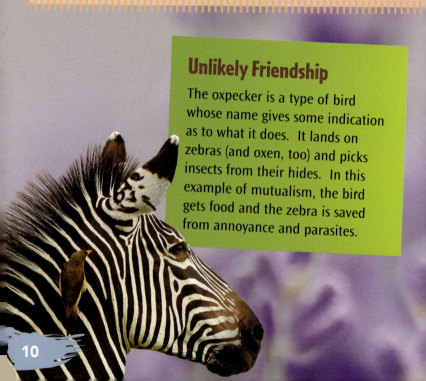

Unlikely Friendship

The oxpecker is a type of bird whose name gives some indication as to what it does. It lands on zebras (and oxen, too) and picks insects from their hides. In this example of mutualism, the bird gets food and the zebra is saved from annoyance and parasites.

Spider crabs and algae have a mutualistic relationship. Look at the photo in the circle. You can see algae living on a crab's back. This helps the crab blend in and gives the algae a place to live. Think about what you see, and consider these questions:

❯ What would happen to the crab if there were no algae? What would happen to the algae if there was no crab?

❯ Does either partner benefit more than the other?

Commensalism

A relationship between two species in which one benefits and the other is neither helped nor harmed is known as *commensalism*. It can be found in many places in nature. Monarch butterflies and milkweeds are a good example.

Colorful monarchs catch the eye of **predators**. But predators avoid monarchs. They know that these butterflies taste bad. Monarchs feed on milkweed. A **toxin** in the plant is harmful to many vertebrates. Monarchs are not harmed by it, and they store it in their body. The act of the monarch storing the toxin benefits the butterfly, but it does not help or hurt the milkweed.

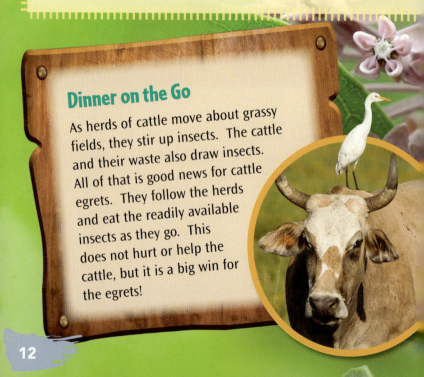

Dinner on the Go

As herds of cattle move about grassy fields, they stir up insects. The cattle and their waste also draw insects. All of that is good news for cattle egrets. They follow the herds and eat the readily available insects as they go. This does not hurt or help the cattle, but it is a big win for the egrets!

Can I Get a Ride?

Emperor shrimp are easy prey because they move so slowly. They catch rides on passing sea cucumbers. In this way, they can easily get from food source to food source without any trouble, and they are protected as they go. Sea cucumbers barely notice their presence.

Predation

Predation is the relationship of predators and prey. One animal lives, and the other dies. Prey do not benefit in predation, but an ecosystem may. Predators keep prey from becoming too **populous**. Too many of one species is not good and can hurt other species.

For example, rabbits reproduce quickly and in big numbers. They can overrun the plant life if their numbers are not kept in check. Predators, such as wolves, eat rabbits. They keep rabbit numbers down. This helps keep the ecosystem in balance.

We Are What We Eat

All animals can be classified into three types of **consumers.** Some animals are herbivores. That means they only eat plants. Sheep, deer, and cows are all herbivores. Meat eaters are carnivores. Lions and sharks are carnivores. Animals that eat both plants and animals are omnivores. Pigs and bears are omnivores.

When a predator feeds off a living host, the predator is called a *parasite*. In this relationship, the parasite is benefited and the host is harmed. A mosquito is a parasite. When it bites a human, a small, red bump appears. The bump is the place where the mosquito drank the human's blood.

Competition

The most harmful relationship to the health of an ecosystem may be *competition*. Neither species benefits from this relationship. Both are harmed.

Each species has a **niche** in nature. But species compete when resources are scarce. This may be due to natural causes, such as fires or floods. It may also happen through human involvement, such as when trees are cut to build homes.

Both species need the resource, and they fight for it. One species wins and takes ownership of the resource. The other species may die out. While mutual, commensal, and predatory relationships help keep an ecosystem balanced, competition does not.

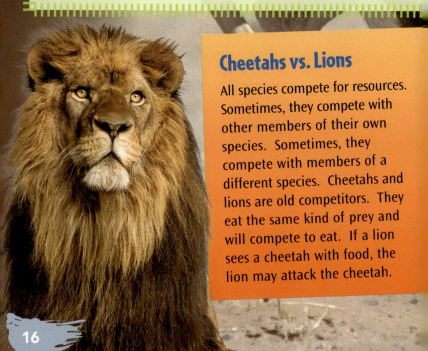

Cheetahs vs. Lions

All species compete for resources. Sometimes, they compete with other members of their own species. Sometimes, they compete with members of a different species. Cheetahs and lions are old competitors. They eat the same kind of prey and will compete to eat. If a lion sees a cheetah with food, the lion may attack the cheetah.

Biotic and Abiotic

All things in an ecosystem are either *biotic* or *abiotic*. Biotic things are living. These can include plants and animals. Abiotic things are not living. These include water, soil, and sunlight.

Human Factor

If humans enter an ecosystem and take the resources that other living things need—such as land—competition begins. Most often, humans win. But scientists say the win is only for the short term. The damage done to the ecosystem creates an **imbalance** that has far-reaching effects.

Humans are part of a **dynamic** web of biotic and abiotic things. When one piece of the web is changed, everything is affected. The full effects may take time to see, but they cannot be avoided. Humans are an important part of the world, and they need resources, too. But balance is key.

Community Ecology

Community ecologists watch how species in an ecosystem interact. They look at what role each species plays. They also track changes in biotic lives.

A Niche for One

No two species can exist in the same niche for a long period of time. The species will fight for the resources there. One of the species will eventually become extinct.

Natural Selection

Each living species is made of **traits** found in its **DNA**. Those qualities determine all aspects of how a species looks and its instincts. Over time, traits change as they **adapt** to the species' environment.

The traits that help the species thrive are the ones that survive into future generations. When these traits are passed onto offspring, it is known as *heredity*. This is nature's way of selecting healthy traits that do well in the world. That is why this process is called *natural selection*.

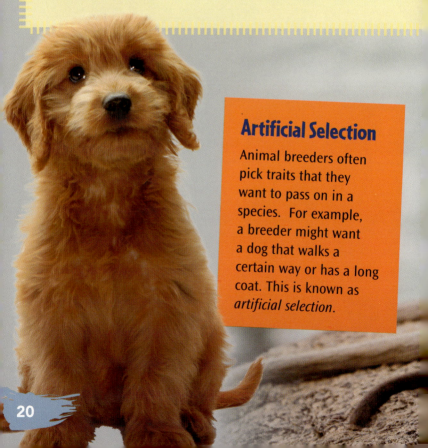

Artificial Selection

Animal breeders often pick traits that they want to pass on in a species. For example, a breeder might want a dog that walks a certain way or has a long coat. This is known as *artificial selection*.

Heredity

Heredity is the process by which traits are passed to offspring. For instance, the color of your hair, your eyes, and your skin are all traits. These, along with many more traits, are passed down to you from your **biological** parents through heredity.

Survival of the Fittest

Organisms and traits that are most suited for an environment are the ones that survive. Organisms reproduce and their traits are passed on to future generations. This is what is meant by "survival of the fittest."

The drawings below depict survival of the fittest. The phrase was first used to explain trait adaptations. Understanding survival of the fittest is key to understanding competition among species. It is through adaptation that the fit survive.

At first, there is enough food for everybody.

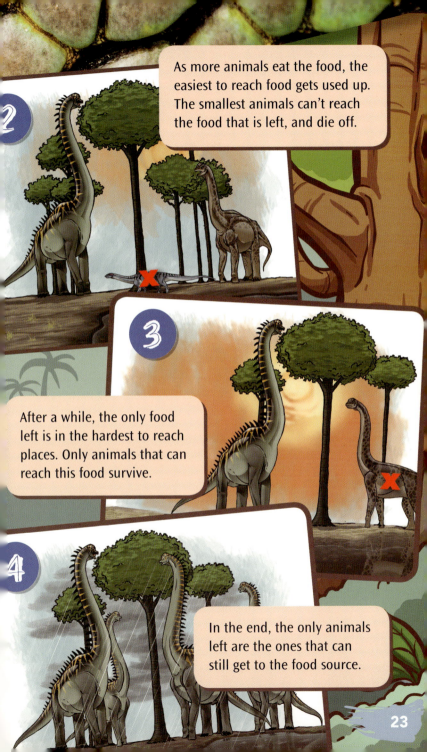

2 As more animals eat the food, the easiest to reach food gets used up. The smallest animals can't reach the food that is left, and die off.

3 After a while, the only food left is in the hardest to reach places. Only animals that can reach this food survive.

4 In the end, the only animals left are the ones that can still get to the food source.

23

Showdown: Inside Habitats

Who would win in a habitat that is shared by both humans and animals? The first step in predicting a winner is to explore the relationships among species. Then, look at other habitats to see how those relationships play out. Think about what happens in habitats as humans compete for resources. Humans always have an impact. More than that, humans are the only species who can figure out how to make a system work for other species.

No other species can predict the impact of its choices the way humans can. In fact, most species cannot make choices at all. Humans have that freedom. And with freedom comes responsibility.

Moral Monkeys

Many scientists study animals to see if they can make **moral** choices. One study was done on a group of monkeys that learned to push a lever to get food. Later on, the monkeys learned that when they pushed the lever, another monkey would get an electric shock. After that, the monkeys refused to push the lever—even if they were very hungry.

Empathetic Elephants

Some people wonder if animals other than humans have empathy. Empathy is the ability to feel what another person or thing feels. One story about elephants says that an old woman with poor eyesight got lost in a jungle. Elephants covered her with branches to keep her safe. They also stood guard until help came.

Chaparral

A chaparral is a habitat in which cool ocean air meets a hot landmass. The area may be flat, hilly, or mountainous. It is often very hot and dry for about half the year. The rest of the year is wet. The long, dry period may result in wildfires.

A chaparral's climate is appealing to many living things. This habitat is common in California, where coastal land is costly to own. Many people move to chaparrals, where land is more affordable and the weather is still pleasant. But as more and more people move there, they create problems.

Space Invaders

During much of the year, days can be hot in chaparrals. Many of the animals there are nocturnal. They sleep during the hottest part of the day and roam at night. The areas around people's houses in chaparrals may be overrun with lizards, rabbits, chipmunks, and more. Each species finds food wherever it can. Often, this means invading human space.

Water Blues

Animals and plants in chaparrals must live with little water. This is one of the biggest challenges of life in chaparrals. People tend to use most of the water. That makes life harder for the other species in the habitat.

Not so long ago, many chaparrals were just open land. Then, animals became **displaced** as people developed this land.

Now, human interactions disturb the wildlife in the area. People bring in non-native plants. They grow lawns and keep flowering plants that use more water than the area has. People try to maintain ways of life that they enjoyed in different habitats. The result is an overuse of resources. It causes displacement of species as their land is overrun. They have nowhere else to go. The animals and humans vie for the same space and resources. There is not enough for everyone. Some species will lose the battle.

Every Continent

Chaparrals can be found all over the world. The West Coast of the United States is home to many chaparral habitats. They can also be found in Chile, South Africa (pictured right), and Australia.

Pollution

As more people move into chaparrals, they bring pollution. Pollution is anything that makes land, water, or air unsafe to use. Even the smallest amount of pollution will harm the wildlife that live there.

Rain Forest

The world's rain forests are lush habitats filled with a variety of animal and plant life. **Precipitation** and **transpiration** are high there.

Rain forests benefit people in many ways. They provide much of the world's oxygen. They are also a source for many medicines. But over the years, many rain forests have been cut down. The trees are used for lumber, and the land is cleared for farming. In the process, animals lose their homes. Many species have become endangered, and some have become extinct. Experts think droughts that have begun in the area are a result of deforestation.

Efforts are being made to stop the heavy deforestation. But progress is slow, and forests continue to fall.

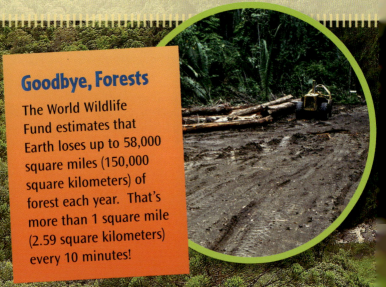

Goodbye, Forests

The World Wildlife Fund estimates that Earth loses up to 58,000 square miles (150,000 square kilometers) of forest each year. That's more than 1 square mile (2.59 square kilometers) every 10 minutes!

Animals at Risk

Around 8 out of 10 of the world's known species live in rain forests. Deforestation puts a high number of those animals at risk.

Carbon-Based Life

Every living thing is made in part of **carbon**, which is found in the land, sea, and sky. Humans and many animals breathe out a gas called **carbon dioxide** (1). Plants use this gas to make their food. In turn, plants release oxygen (2), which many animals (including humans) breathe.

As people use resources, the balance of carbon in the atmosphere and in ecosystems is affected (3). This changes the climate and, therefore, affects animals as well. In the short term, humans benefit. But in the long term, whole ecosystems are altered. Animals must adapt or die.

Causes of Climate Change

Rain forest plants help to balance gas levels in the atmosphere. As large areas of rain forest are cut down, gas levels shift and the planet warms up. This leads to **climate change**.

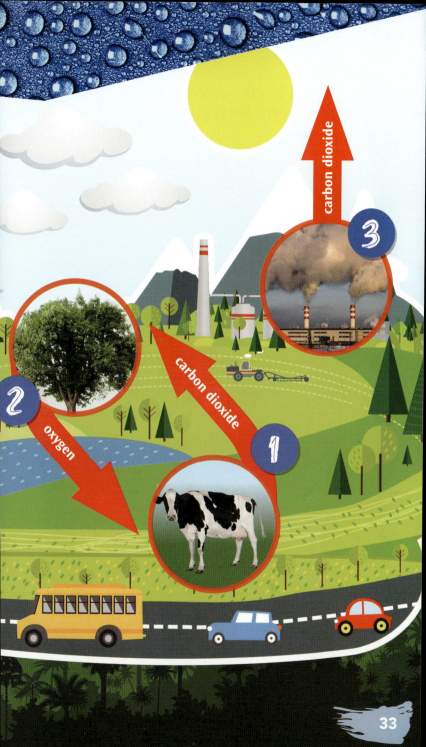

carbon dioxide

carbon dioxide

oxygen

3

2

1

Ocean

Most of Earth is covered by oceans. Humans are not ocean animals, but they rely on ocean resources. In particular, they use sea animals as food sources.

For many years, Atlantic cod was a major food source. Many fishers made their livings catching cod. The ocean was filled with cod, and they stayed high on the food chain. Cod fed freely on other fish and helped to maintain the balance of the ecosystem. Their enormous size made many **fisheries** wealthy. But the demand for cod almost completely destroyed the species.

World's Largest

The ocean is the world's largest **biome**. It covers about 70 percent of Earth's surface. There are over one million species of plants and animals that live in the ocean. Scientists predict that there are millions more species that have not yet been discovered.

Coral Reefs

The ocean is the most **diverse** biome on Earth. Many ocean species find homes in coral reefs. Some studies suggest that 1 out of 4 ocean animals rely on coral reefs for food and shelter.

Humans **depleted** cod through overfishing. It reached a point that the cod could not recover. They could not reproduce in numbers big enough to allow some cod to grow to their full size. Many young cod were being eaten. Consequently, cod shrank in size, and they lost their place in the food chain.

Many fisheries have since collapsed. People have lost their jobs. The cod are still adapting to a new niche, as is everything in the ecosystem—including humans.

Unemployed

The cod industry had grown over the years. Then, in the 1990s, it collapsed. In a single day, more than 40,000 fishers in Canada lost their jobs.

Apex Predator

The cod was once an *apex predator*, meaning it was at the top of the food chain. After it lost its position in the food chain, the population of its prey consequently exploded.

Grasslands

Grasslands are marked by fields of grasses. Limited rainfall keeps many trees from growing. Large groups of animals make grasslands their home. Today, the land is often used for farming.

In North America, bison roamed the grasslands for many years. They were a major food source for American Indians. When European settlers came to the land, they hunted the bison almost to extinction.

The newcomers also wiped out many American Indians. They took away their food source and their land. American Indian numbers decreased. Their lives were changed forever.

Rabbit Trouble

In 1859, about 25 rabbits were brought from England to Australia. At the time, there were no rabbits there. Since then, they have overtaken the land. They have changed ecosystems. Many plants and animals have become endangered through competing with rabbits for resources.

By Any Other Name

Grasslands are called *savannahs* in Africa. They are known as *rangelands* in Australia. Go to South America, and grasslands are called *llanos*. And in North America, grasslands are called *plains*.

All Connected

No species lives apart from others. The activity of every species has an effect on the whole ecosystem. And because ecosystems are connected, the whole planet is altered.

Competition is natural among some species. Life adapts. Some species get stronger. Others fall away. But sometimes, things happen beyond what is natural. Usually, these things happen at the hands of people. Humans often use more resources than they need. They may build and develop without care for other species and resources.

We know that what humans do affects not only other species but other humans, too. The impact may not be felt right away. But it *will* be felt, because all things in life are connected.

Constant Competition

Humans are in constant competition with small creatures. Some of these creatures use the same resources humans do. Flies, ants, and mosquitoes compete with humans for resources, such as space and food.

Butterfly Effect

The *butterfly effect* is a theory, which says that a small event in one place can have a huge impact somewhere else. The idea is that a butterfly might flap its wings and set off a chain reaction with massive results. Even a small event may have a big consequence.

Glossary

adapt—to change something to make it easier to live in an area

biological—used to describe parents who gave birth to a child

biome—a large community of plants and animals that live in a single place

carbon—a chemical element that is found in all living plants and animals

carbon dioxide—a colorless, odorless gas that is absorbed by plants to make food.

climate change—the recent increase in the world's temperature

consumers—organisms that feed on other organisms

depleted—used most or all of something

displaced—removed from the usual or proper place

diverse—made up of many different unlike elements

DNA—substance that carries a living thing's hereditary information

dynamic—always changing

ecosystems—all living and nonliving things in a particular environment

fisheries—businesses that catch and sell fish

habitat—the type of place where a plant or animal normally or naturally grows or lives

imbalance—a state in which things do not occur in equal or normal amounts

instinct—a way of behaving, feeling, or thinking that is natural and not learned

moral—concerned with what is right and wrong in human behavior

niche—an area where a species is best suited to survive

precipitation—water that falls to the ground as rain or snow

predators—animals that eat other animals as their food source

prey—animal that is hunted by other animals as their food source

reproduction—the process that results in new babies, animals, or plants

resources—things that provide something useful and necessary

toxin— a poison or venom of plant or animal origin

traits—characteristics that make one person or thing different from another

transpiration—the transfer of water from plants to the atmosphere

vie—to compete with others in an attempt to get something

Index

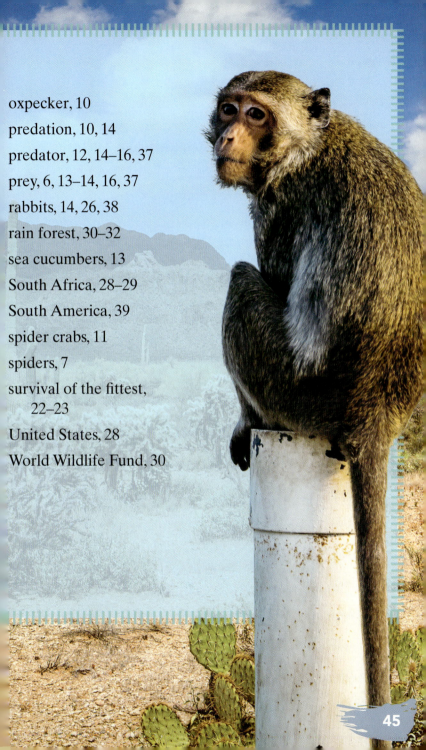

Check It Out!

Books

Burnie, David. 2011. *Eyewitness Plant*. DK Children.

Hopkinson, Deborah. 2005. *Who Was Charles Darwin?* Grosset & Dunlap.

National Geographic Kids. 2012. *125 True Stories of Amazing Animals*. National Geographic Children's Books.

Rice, William B. 2016. *Life and Non-Life in an Ecosystem*. Teacher Created Materials.

Rice, William B. 2016. *Life and the Flow of Energy*. Teacher Created Materials.

Videos

National Geographic Crittercam. www.animals. nationalgeographic.com/animals/crittercam/

Websites

BioExpedition. www.bioexpedition.com

National Geographic Kids. www.kids.nationalgeographic.com

World Wildlife Fund (WWF). www.worldwildlife.org

Try It!

You've just landed your dream job of working to protect animal habitats. But on your first day, there is already a huge problem! A company just bought a large piece of land where animals live, and they plan to turn the land into a shopping mall. It is up to you to save the animals!

- Draw a picture of the land that is being bought. Make sure to label areas where animals live.

- Try to determine if there is a way to share the land between the animals and the company. If so, draw your plan for the land. If not, think of ways to convince the company to build something that helps, not harms, the animals.

- Write a letter to the company asking them to follow your plan. Be sure to include your drawing with your letter.

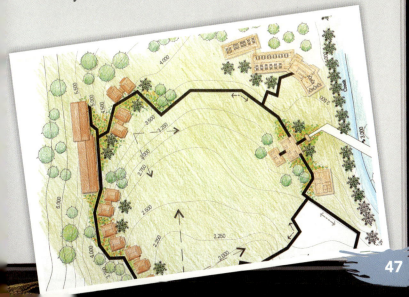

About the Author

Dona Herweck Rice has written hundreds of books, stories, and essays for kids on all kinds of topics, from pirates to why some people have bad breath! Writing is her passion. But she also loves reading, dancing, and singing at the top of her lungs (although she'd be the first to tell you that this is not really a pleasure for anyone else). Rice was a teacher and is an acting coach. She lives in Southern California with her husband, two sons, and a cute but very silly dog.

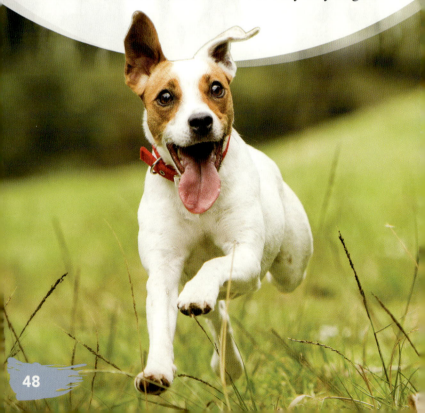